To:

_____

From:

_____

A GIANT HEADACHE

The Story of David and Goliath

Written and Illustrated by Paul & Delores Gully

BroadStreet
KIDS

Published by BroadStreet Kids
BroadStreet Kids is an imprint of

BroadStreet Publishing® Group, LLC
Savage, Minnesota USA
BroadStreetPublishing.com

A Giant Headache: The Story of David & Goliath

Written and illustrated by Paul & Delores Gully

ISBN 978-1-4245-5641-0 (hardcover)
ISBN 978-1-4245-5722-6 (ebook)

Stock or custom editions of BroadStreet Publishing titles may be purchased in bulk for educational, business, ministry, fundraising, or sales promotional use. For information, please e-mail info@broadstreetpublishing.com.

Printed in China

18 19 20 21   5 4 3 2 1

This true story
is from
1 Samuel 17
in the Bible.

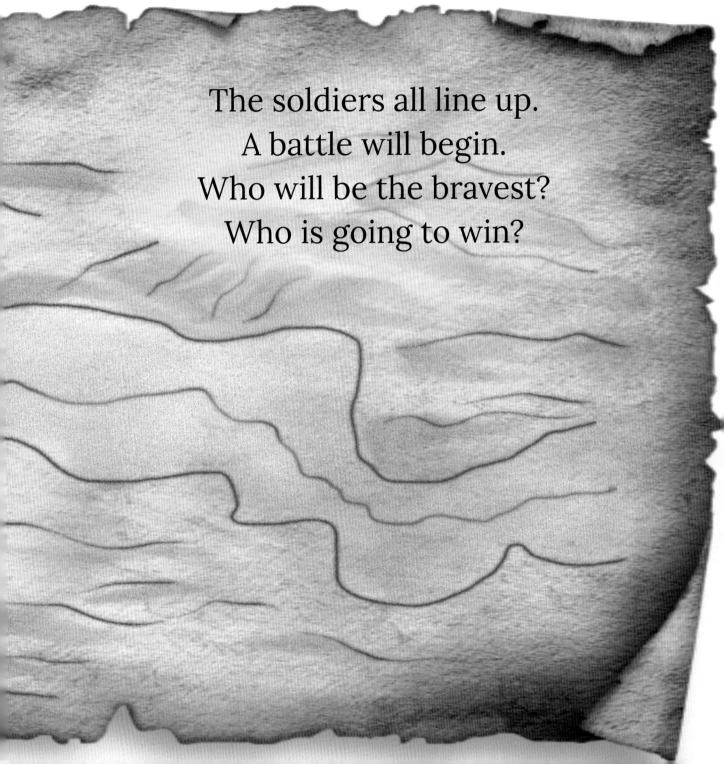

The soldiers all line up.
A battle will begin.
Who will be the bravest?
Who is going to win?

The Philistines cheer their hero,
standing ten feet tall.
The giant called Goliath
drove fear into all.

For forty days and nights,
Goliath stomped and yelled,
"No one wants to fight me?
You cowards of Israel!"

A shepherd boy named David
lived on a farm nearby.
He cared for all his sheep,
and sang to God Most High.

With orders from his father
and cheese that had a smell,
he went to find his brothers
and heard Goliath yell.

David asked the soldiers,
"Why will no one fight?"
His brother then accused him,
"Your heart is just not right."

So David told King Saul,
"He mocks the Lord on High.
Someone stop that giant!
If you let me, I will try."

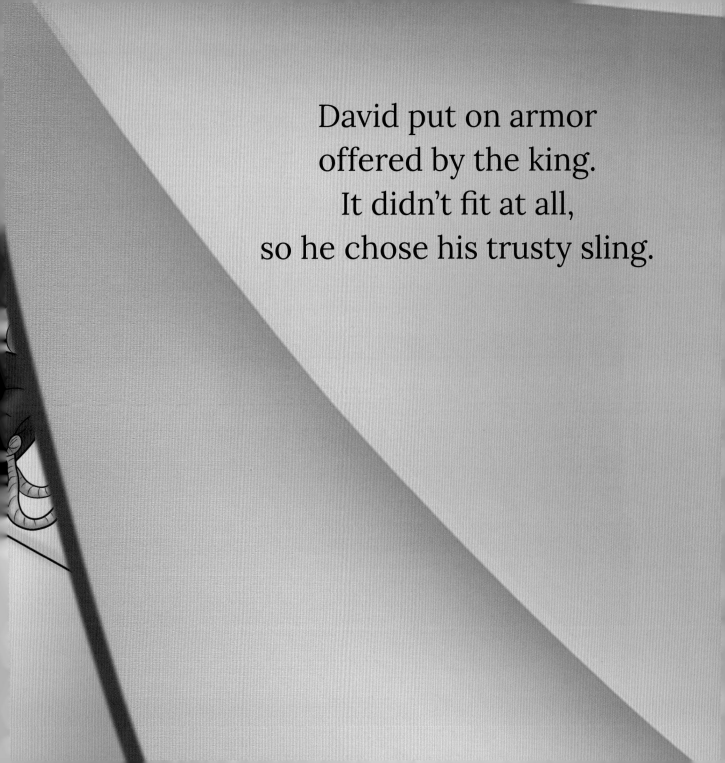

David put on armor
offered by the king.
It didn't fit at all,
so he chose his trusty sling.

He picked up five smooth stones
as he crossed the brook.
He bravely met the giant
who had an angry look.

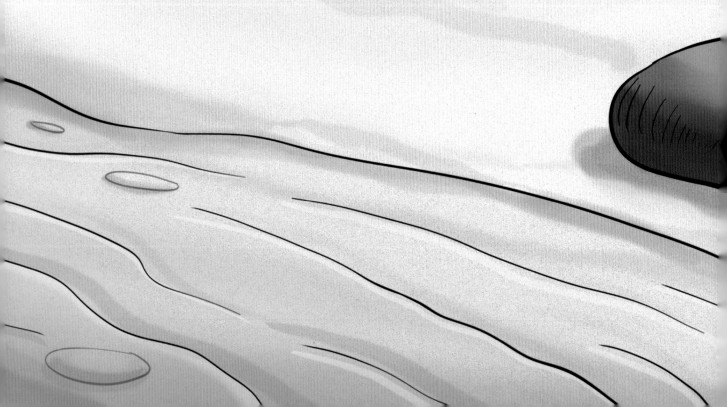

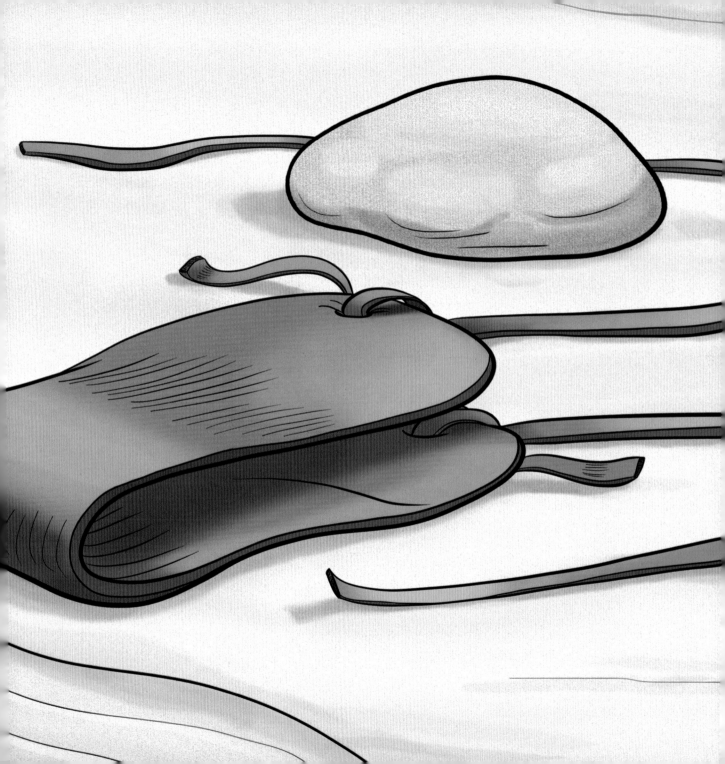

Goliath laughed at David.
"Your army sent a boy?"
The giant's laugh grew louder,
"Your sling is just a toy!"

David loaded up his sling,
trusting God was there.
He spun a stone around,
and flung it through the air.

The armies watched the stone
and to everyone's surprise,
it struck the mean, old giant
right between the eyes.

God's blessings were on David,
who one day would be king.
Our greater King is coming–
JESUS! Lord of everything.

So do not fear your battles,
or giants who stomp and yell.
As God made David brave,
he'll make you strong as well.

If you'd like to know God's plan for
your life and be his special child,
say this simple prayer to God called

The ABC Prayer.

 **ADMIT:**
Admit that you are a sinner.
(That means you have done wrong things.)

 BELIEVE:
Believe that Jesus is God's only Son, and he chose to
die on a cross for the wrong things you've done.

 COMMIT:
Commit to Jesus as Lord
(that means he is first place in your life),
and confess that to others
(confess means to tell people).

God loved

_____

so much that he gave
his only Son, so that if

_____

believes in him,

_____

will not die, but

_____

will have life forever.

JOHN 3:16

WRITE YOUR NAME IN THE SPACES OF THIS BIBLE VERSE

Paul and Delores Gully currently reside in the mountains of Dillard, Georgia. They met while attending Ringling College of Art and Design where Delores mistook Paul for one of his identical triplet brothers, who was in her class. Their God-given talent has been utilized to illustrate books and curriculum worldwide. Their passion is to help children understand how much God loves them. They enjoy traveling, hiking, fishing, reading, bicycling, and watching action movies.

Connect with the Gullys at PaulGullyIllustrator.com and Facebook.com/pvggraphicsanddesign.

Enjoy another great Bible story!

The Big Flood is the biblical story of Noah and the great flood in a rhyming, fun format. It teaches how we can trust God even when we don't understand, so we can carry out his big plan.

The Story of Noah and the Ark

THE
BIG
FLOOD

Written and Illustrated by Paul & Delores Gully

God loved a man named Noah,
and Noah loved God too.
God had big plans for Noah.
What do you think he'll do?